Elizabeth I

Stephanie Turnbull

Designed by Laura Parker

Illustrated by Colin King

Additional illustrations by Adam Larkum

Elizabethan consultant: Heather Thomas

Reading consultant: Alison Kelly,
Roehampton University

Contents

Elizabeth's England

Elizabeth I ruled England about 400 years ago. The people who lived at that time are called Elizabethans.

Most Elizabethans lived in villages in the countryside.

Many ordinary people worked as farmers. They were very poor.

The royal family

Elizabeth was born in 1533. Her father was King Henry VIII and her mother was Anne Boleyn.

This is a painting of Henry in his finest clothes, decorated with expensive jewels.

Henry married six times. Anne was his second wife.

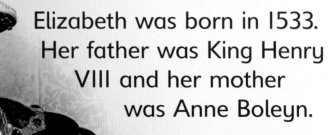

This is a painting of Anne Boleyn.

Henry became angry with her and had her killed when Elizabeth was two.

Two of Henry's other wives had children, so Elizabeth had a half-sister and a half-brother.

Mary was much older than Elizabeth.

Edward was the youngest child.

Growing up

Henry sent Elizabeth to live in Hatfield Palace, near London.

Elizabeth lived with her brother, Edward, and lots of servants.

Teachers gave her lessons. She worked hard and learned fast.

She also learned to dance, sing and play musical instruments.

Elizabeth enjoyed going for long rides on her horse.

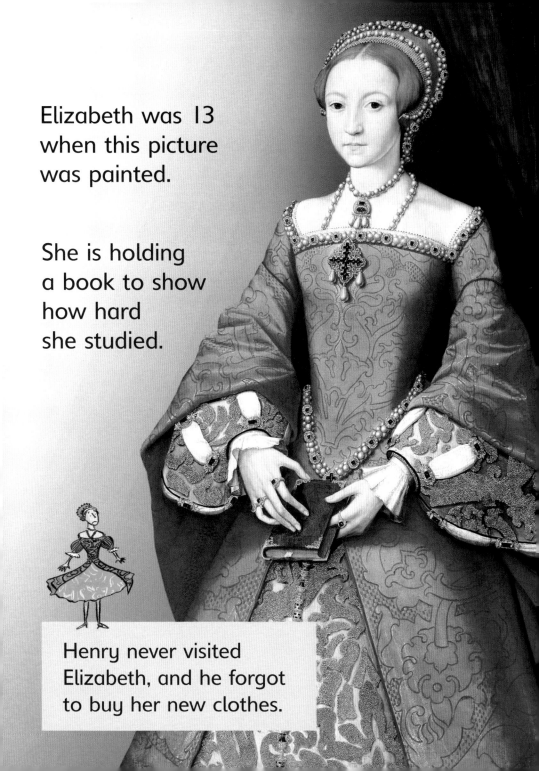

Elizabeth was 13 when this picture was painted.

She is holding a book to show how hard she studied.

Henry never visited Elizabeth, and he forgot to buy her new clothes.

Edward and Mary

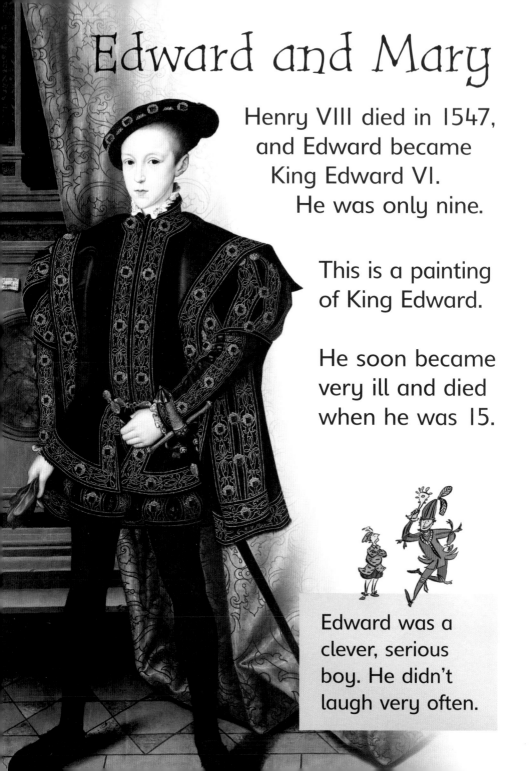

Henry VIII died in 1547, and Edward became King Edward VI. He was only nine.

This is a painting of King Edward.

He soon became very ill and died when he was 15.

Edward was a clever, serious boy. He didn't laugh very often.

When Edward died, Elizabeth's sister Mary became Queen Mary 1.

Mary's advisers told her that Elizabeth was plotting to be Queen instead.

Mary sent the terrified Elizabeth to prison in the Tower of London.

Later, Elizabeth was allowed to go home, but guards watched her closely.

A new life

In 1558, Mary died. Suddenly Elizabeth's life changed forever – she was the new Queen.

Huge crowds cheered as Elizabeth was made Queen in London.

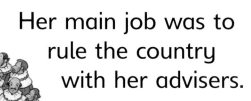

Her main job was to rule the country with her advisers.

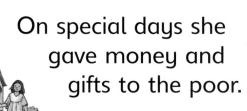

On special days she gave money and gifts to the poor.

Elizabeth had more than 60 palaces. This is Hampton Court, where she often stayed.

Elizabeth had so many homes that she gave them to friends as presents.

The Queen's court

All kinds of servants, advisers and courtiers lived with Elizabeth at her court.

Courtiers entertained the Queen and gave her presents.

They often had picnics with her in the countryside.

This painting shows Elizabeth dancing with a courtier.

Sometimes, courtiers had contests called jousts for Elizabeth to watch.

In a joust, each man used a lance to try to push the other man off his horse.

Elizabeth gave a prize to the winner. This was usually a sparkling jewel.

Dressing up

Elizabethans liked to dress well. The Queen's clothes were the most magnificent of all.

First, servants helped Elizabeth put on underwear.

Next, she wore a stiff, wide skirt with a dress over the top.

Then, servants added sleeves and lots of stiff frills.

For going out, she put on a thick cloak, gloves and a hat.

Rich ladies liked to have pale skin, so Elizabeth always painted her face white.

She had jewels sewn onto her clothes.

Elizabethans hardly ever had baths. They carried perfume to hide their smell.

A royal feast

Elizabeth had many visitors. She impressed them with huge, expensive feasts.

Glittering salt containers like this one often stood on the tables.

A feast began with meat and fish.

It ended with sweet tarts and cakes.

The most important
guests sat with
the Queen.

Servants rushed
from table to table
with food and wine.

Musicians played
tunes and acrobats
made people laugh.

Elizabeth ate so many sweet
things that her teeth rotted.

London life

The city of London grew fast in Elizabethan times. Elizabeth had many palaces there.

Ordinary people lived in crowded houses on narrow, dirty streets.

The River Thames was a busy place. All kinds of boats sailed up and down it.

There was just one bridge across the river. Tall houses were built all along it.

This painting shows courtiers carrying Elizabeth through London. The Queen's chair is called a litter.

London was so dirty that many people caught horrible diseases.

19

Watching plays

Many Elizabethans, including the Queen, loved to see plays.

Plays were shown in playhouses like this one, which was called the Globe.

One section has been cut away so you can see inside.

Everyone had to pay at the door to see the play.

People often bought food to eat inside the playhouse.

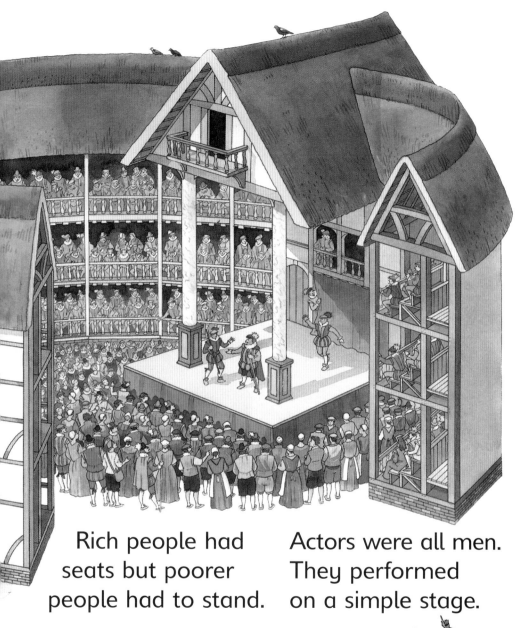

Rich people had seats but poorer people had to stand.

Actors were all men. They performed on a simple stage.

People standing in the crowd often threw food at bad actors.

21

A rival queen

Elizabeth had an enemy, Mary Stuart, who was the Queen of Scotland.

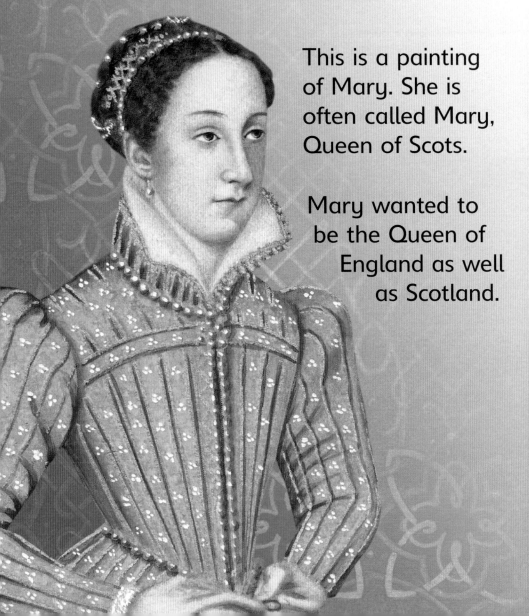

This is a painting of Mary. She is often called Mary, Queen of Scots.

Mary wanted to be the Queen of England as well as Scotland.

Elizabeth locked Mary up to keep her out of the way.

Mary's friends planned to free her and kill Elizabeth.

They sent secret letters to Mary, hidden in barrels.

Elizabeth's spies found the letters and Mary was killed.

Elizabeth and Mary had spies to find out what each other was up to.

Explorers

Many Elizabethan sailors
explored the world.

Francis Drake sailed
around the world
in a ship just like
this one, called
the Golden Hinde.

Wind blew
into the sails
and pushed
the ship along.

Francis Drake set off on his trip around the world in 1577.

He came back three years later with gold, silver and jewels.

This is a painting of Walter Raleigh, an explorer who went to America.

Walter Raleigh brought the first potatoes to England. People tried to eat them raw!

Fighting at sea

English explorers often stole treasure from Spanish ships. King Philip of Spain was furious.

1. Philip sent more than 100 warships to attack England.

2. Elizabeth quickly sent English ships to fight with them.

3. There was a huge sea battle and the Spanish turned back.

4. Storms destroyed many Spanish ships as they sailed home.

This old picture of the battle shows many Spanish warships on fire.

Fighting ships had cannons on board that fired big metal balls.

27

The Queen dies

As Elizabeth got older, she often felt tired and ill. She died in 1603, aged 69.

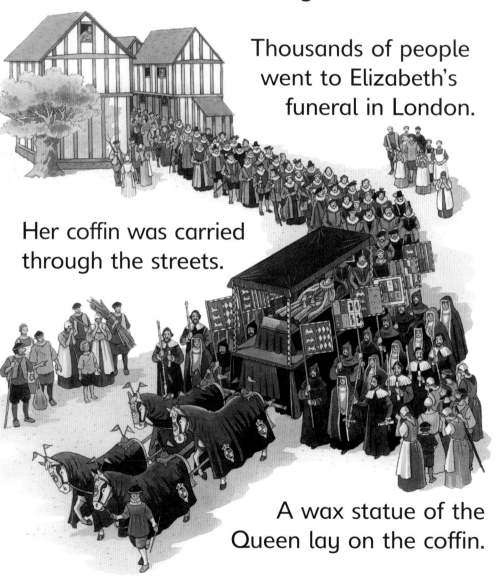

Thousands of people went to Elizabeth's funeral in London.

Her coffin was carried through the streets.

A wax statue of the Queen lay on the coffin.

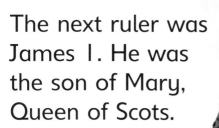

The next ruler was James I. He was the son of Mary, Queen of Scots.

This picture of James was probably painted when he had just become King.

King James loved to spend money, especially on clothes.

Glossary of useful words

Here are some of the words in this book you might not know. This page tells you what they mean.

 adviser - someone who gives advice. Elizabeth had advisers to help her rule.

 plotting - planning something in secret, for example how to beat an enemy.

 Tower of London - a palace that was also a prison. It still stands today.

 court - wherever a king or queen and their servants and courtiers were living.

 courtier - a rich person who lived with a king or queen at court.

 joust - a game where two men tried to knock each other off their horses.

 lance - a long pole that was used as a weapon in a joust.

Websites to visit

If you have a computer, you can find out more about Elizabeth I on the Internet. On the Usborne Quicklinks Website there are links to four fun websites.

Website 1 - Look at different paintings of Queen Elizabeth I.

Website 2 - Dress an Elizabethan doll.

Website 3 - Choose a horse and test your jousting skills in a great game.

Website 4 - Print out lots of Elizabethan pictures to shade in.

To visit these websites, go to **www.usborne-quicklinks.com** Read the Internet safety guidelines, and then type the keywords "beginners Elizabeth".

The websites are regularly reviewed and the links in Usborne Quicklinks are updated. However, Usborne Publishing is not responsible, and does not accept liability, for the content or availability of any website other than its own. We recommend that children are supervised while on the Internet.

Index

Acknowledgements

Photographic manipulation by Mike Wheatley

Photo credits

The publishers are grateful to the following for permission to reproduce material:
© **The Art Archive** 1 (Victoria and Albert Museum/Sally Chappell), 27 (University Library Geneva/Dagli Orti);
© **The Bridgeman Art Library** 4 (Belvoir Castle), 5 (Hever Castle), 19 (Private Collection),
25 (Kunsthistorisches Museum, Vienna); © **Corbis** 11 (Sandro Vannini), 22 (Michael Nicholson), 24 (Joel W.
Rogers), 29 (Gianni Dagli Orti); © **The National Maritime Museum, London** 15; © **The National Portrait
Gallery, London** cover; **The Royal Collection © 2004, Her Majesty Queen Elizabeth II** 7, 8, 16;
© **The Trustees of the British Museum,** 31;
and 12 reproduced by kind permission of Viscount De L'Isle, from his private collection.